Dudmaston

Shropshire

 THE NATIONAL TRUST

Ancient and modern

DUDMASTON looks, at first sight, like a thousand other English country houses. The plain red sandstone building sits quietly and comfortably in traditional English parkland. The dark panelled Entrance Hall has changed little since it was created in the early 18th century. But in this room, one gets a first hint of something different: hanging on equal terms among the expected family portraits is a large painting of one of the Dudmaston gamekeepers.

An integrated estate

Dudmaston is not just a historic house and garden, but a model of an integrated agricultural estate, which has never been sold since it was first acquired by the Wolryche family in 1403. The crest of the Wolryches is an oak-tree – a highly appropriate symbol, as succeeding generations have particularly cherished the Dudmaston woodland, which still preserves fragments of the ancient Forest of Morfe.

Making Dudmaston modern

Even more unusually, the house and the garden are filled with bold examples of contemporary art. What other estate with a 600-year history can claim to have enjoyed its most exciting phase in the last 35 years? When Sir GEORGE and RACHEL, LADY LABOUCHERE retired to live at Dudmaston in 1966, they set about bringing the place back to life by cheerful redecoration. They introduced displays of historic furniture, pictures and ceramics inherited by Lady Labouchere, mixed with 20th-century paintings and sculpture collected by Sir George. They did all this, while at the same time overseeing the generous handover of the estate to the National Trust, finally achieved in 1978. The Laboucheres made modern Dudmaston, and made it modern.

Ups and downs

In Dudmaston's long history, this is just the latest in a series of bursts of prosperity and activity, which have interrupted long periods of tranquil decline, when money was short. In the late 17th century Sir THOMAS WOLRYCHE, 3rd Bt began building the present house, but died in 1701 before he could see it finished. The architect was probably Francis Smith, a prolific local builder who was more reliable than inspired.

Sir Thomas's wayward son John almost bankrupted the family, before also dying young in a drunken accident in 1723. Little further happened until 1775, when WILLIAM WHITMORE inherited the estate. He set about modernising the antiquated agricultural estate

Coquillage; by Max Ernst, 1961. From the Laboucheres' modern art collection (© ADAGP, Paris and DACS, London 2002)

'Complete with its woods, village and farms (all owned together for so long and affected by the interweaving threads of national events), Dudmaston Estate spells out the hundreds of years of local history, which is now more than ever desirable to show as evidence of the evolution of rural communities up to our present time.... We wish to emphasise that the full value for the future that it has to offer to the public will be achieved only if it is kept substantially as a whole.'

Rachel, Lady Labouchere

(Left) The entrance front

with vigour. This process of improvement was taken up even more actively by his son, WILLIAM WOLRYCHE-WHITMORE, who was the only member of the family to make a mark in national life, campaigning in Parliament for the removal of restrictions on international free trade. Unfortunately, the estate had to be mortgaged to pay for his improvements – mortgages that were not finally paid off until the end of the 19th century. The next revival began in 1908, when GEOFFREY WOLRYCHE-WHITMORE took over the estate. He devoted his energies to making Dudmaston a pioneer in modern forestry methods. In the 1960s the Laboucheres masterminded the most recent renaissance, which has made Dudmaston such an unusual and fascinating place. Dudmaston remains a family home, cherished by Lady Labouchere's cousin, Col. James Hamilton-Russell, and his family.

Tour of the House

The Entrance Hall

The Entrance Hall has changed little since Sir Thomas Wolryche's new house was completed in the early 18th century. It still has its original panelling, which was designed to give the room a classical grandeur. However, the local craftsmen responsible were not quite abreast of the latest fashion. The side-doors have slightly squat proportions, and the pediment hangs rather awkwardly over the central double-doors opposite the entrance. These double-doors would once have led into the main reception rooms on the garden side of the house, but were blocked up in the 1820s to make the new Library in the room behind (see p. 8).

The plasterwork oval of flowers and fruit on the ceiling is also original, like the stone floor, which has withstood ten generations of country boots.

Pictures

The portrait in the richly carved frame over the fireplace depicts John Wolryche, MP, the father of the builder of the house. He is shown as a soldier, in Roman armour and holding a general's baton. To the left of the double-doors are two more 17th-century portraits: of John's younger brother, Thomas (shown with a churchwarden's pipe; smoking had been introduced to Britain in Elizabethan times); and of John's father, Sir Thomas Wolryche, 1st Bt (shown in armour and with the besieged

The Entrance Hall

The 1692 coat of arms of the Langley family is made from tightly rolled pieces of paper

Bridgnorth Castle behind, of which he was governor during the Civil War in 1643–4).

Dudmaston possesses a particularly interesting group of *portraits of servants*. The unusually large portrait of an early 18th-century Dudmaston gamekeeper (right of the double-doors) may depict George Griffith, the favourite servant of the last Baronet, Sir John Wolryche, who almost ruined the estate by his devotion to hunting and gambling (see p. 26). Griffith may also appear in the large picture of the Wolryche Hunt about 1720, which hangs in the centre of the right-hand wall.

Furniture

The *17th-century oak and elm table* may have come from the earlier Tudor house (see p. 24). One end is incised for use as a shovel-board. The *great chest* in front of the double-doors has been in this room for over 200 years. On it stands the sporting gun used by Col. Thomas Weld, who inherited Dudmaston in 1771.

The other furnishings have been introduced more recently. *The superb set of late 17th-century walnut chairs and two settees* (AIL) was made for the Earl of Nottingham's Burley-on-the-Hill. The vivid colours of their embroidered upholstery have survived only because they have been protected in the traditional way with loose covers. The set was bought by Sir George Labouchere. Flanking the fireplace are *two late 17th-century Dutch dummy boards* of elegantly dressed children. These painted wooden figures are found in many older country houses peopling empty interiors.

On the table beneath the painting of the Wolryche Hunt is a *quillwork hatchment* of the Langley coat of arms dated 23 March 1692. Originally, this intricate technique used bird quills and feathers to create a design, but often – as here – tightly rolled tubes of paper were substituted. Hatchments were diamond-shaped panels made to commemorate a recently deceased member of the family. They were often hung in churches.

The portrait of the so-called 'Wolryche Fool' (perhaps the kitchen-boy 'Jack' mentioned in contemporary accounts) shows him with the glass goblet displayed nearby. It is signed by a local artist, George Alsop, and dated 1719. The same glass apparently features in the portrait over the right-hand door (illustrated on p. 22), again by Alsop, which is said to show the Wolryche Fool when older, but looks nothing like him, and may rather be of another member of the household. His cap is in the same red and blue livery worn by the members of the Wolryche Hunt in the painting on the left.

The Study

Like the Entrance Hall, the Study retains its original panelling. It continues to be used as an office by the tenant, Col. James Hamilton-Russell. On the right is the head of a wild boar killed in 1935 in the Kadir Cup, the all-India pig-sticking championship.

The Staircase Hall

This new staircase was created by John Smalman in the 1820s as part of his remodelling of Dudmaston for William and Lady Lucy Wolryche-Whitmore. Smalman preserved the old wooden doorcases, but added a new polished white marble floor and the stone stairs, which are skilfully cantilevered. The Neoclassical detailing of the metal banisters is especially delicate and precise.

The room was redecorated the present shade of white in 1967, when Sir George and Lady Labouchere retired to live at Dudmaston. The stair-carpet was woven at the same time in nearby Kidderminster, a traditional centre of English carpet-making. It was dyed green to match the shades in Roelandt Savery's *Stag Hunt*, which hangs on the stairs.

Pictures

Several of the paintings recall the Laboucheres' years in the Diplomatic Service. The head-and-shoulders portrait of Victoria in 1837 (the year she became Queen) was copied from Thomas Sully's original full-length by the Irish artist Richard Rothwell. It hung in the British Legation in Budapest and in the embassies in Brussels and Madrid, when the Laboucheres were serving there. The portrait on the staircase of Lady Labouchere in a Hartnell gown was painted in 1962 by the Spanish artist Ricardo Macarron. A reproduction of his 1982 portrait of the Queen hangs under the stairs.

Other pictures here include a Dutch 17th-century portrait of two girls, who must be sisters. One holds striped or 'broken' tulips, which had provoked a craze in Holland in the 1630s. Through the window on the right, one gets a fascinating glimpse into a formal Dutch tulip garden of the period, with paths divided by trellises.

Sculpture

The white marble bust under the stairs is of Lady Lucy Wolryche-Whitmore, for whom this room was remodelled. She was a talented musician, and her Erard harp (bought on 20 March 1817) stands nearby.

Furniture

The *large bronze bell* is inscribed 'I Wolrythe De Dudmaston 1680' (that is, John Wolryche, MP [1637–85], whose portrait also hangs in the Hall). The bell hung in the tower over the back door of the house until it became unsafe, when Geoffrey Wolryche-Whitmore put it in the present frame.

Most of the furnishings came from Adcote, the Shropshire house built in 1879 by Norman Shaw for Lady Labouchere's great-grandmother, Rebecca Darby, and largely furnished by her Christy brothers (see p. 30). They include a Louis XVI kingwood commode, George II chairs, an urn of Derbyshire fluorspar (known as bluejohn), and blue-and-white Kangxi vases. The pair of Egyptian brown porphyry and ormolu vases was made in the Swedish royal factory.

(Left) The striped tulips held by one of the sisters were particularly prized in 17th-century Holland, where this picture was painted

(Right) The Staircase Hall

The Library was redecorated by Nina Campbell in 1967

The Library

In the early 19th century, life in many large country houses became less formal, and as a result libraries were often converted into larger and more sociable sitting rooms. This is what happened here in the 1820s, when Smalman converted two rooms into a large library.

The bookcases, with their decoration of flowers and ears of wheat, were modelled on those at Weston Park, the family home of Lady Lucy Bridgeman before she married William Wolryche-Whitmore in 1810. William had need of more shelving, as he wrote numerous pamphlets on the repeal of the Corn Laws and the other political causes he espoused. He also had a much-used account with a Worcester bookseller, Richard Hill.

The floor-length plate-glass windows were installed in 1833 for Lady Lucy, whose health was always delicate, so that she could enjoy the stunning views over the garden without having to step outside. The English cut-glass chandelier was made specifically for this room in the 1830s. The end window bays were filled by bookcases until 1965, when the Laboucheres moved them upstairs. The early 19th-century carpet is English.

Like the Staircase Hall, the Library was decorated for the Laboucheres in 1967 in white with yellow curtains by Nina Campbell, a protégé of the leading interior decorator John Fowler. This was one of her first independent commissions; she now has a thriving design business in South Kensington. John Ward's watercolour on the near bookcase shows the Laboucheres in the Library with their labrador Katie in 1984.

Flower paintings

Over the fireplace is a signed work by Jan van
Os (1744–1808) which includes brilliantly
observed details of roses, tulips, peonies,
auriculas and fritillaries. To the right is another
flowerpiece (AIL) by Jan van Huysum (1682–
1749). Those on the window wall are by van
Os and Paul Theodorus van Brussel (1754–95).
They were collected by Francis Darby and
hung for many years at Sunniside, his house at
Coalbrookdale. They were brought here in
1966 by Lady Labouchere, who had inherited
them from Muriel Cope Darby.

Improving on nature

The fashion for immaculately painted still-
lifes of flowers developed in Holland in the
early 17th century. By the 18th century,
when the examples shown here were
painted, the floral arrangements had reached
the height of exuberance, with masses of
loose petals and double blooms set against
lighter backgrounds. The results may look
very realistic, but they are in fact highly
artificial, bringing together varieties that
would never have been in bloom together.

Portraits

A portrait of the creator of this room, William
Wolryche-Whitmore, painted about 1810, the
year he married Lady Lucy, hangs over the
entrance door on the near wall. At the right end
of the same wall is one of his sister, Mary
Dorothea, and between them is Lady
Labouchere's grandmother, Lady Katharine
Scott, who married the 8th Viscount Boyne.

On the opposite wall, above the clock, are
images of William's North Country grand-
parents, John and Dorothy Pate-Lister, painted
about 1740. Flanking them are, on the left, Mary
Wolryche, the sister of the dissolute 4th and last
Baronet, and, on the right, Col. Thomas Weld's
illegitimate daughter Mary. Above the bookcases facing the windows are portraits of Sir
Lister Kaye Holte, MP for Lichfield, by Tilly
Kettle, and Col. William Legge, by Jacob
Huysmans. Nicknamed 'Honest Will', Legge
was a devoted supporter of Charles I, being
seriously wounded three times fighting for the
King during the Civil War.

Furniture and ceramics

Most of the furniture is 18th-century French.
The 18th-century chairs in the Chippendale
style and much of the Chinese porcelain came
from Adcote.

9

The Oak Room

Like the Entrance Hall, this cosy little sitting room still has its original panelling. The only important alteration is the marble fireplace, which was installed in the 1970s. The windows were extended to ground level in the 1830s, like all those facing the garden.

Portraits

Right of the entrance door is a portrait of Francis Wolryche, inscribed as painted in 1591, when he was 28, making it the earliest family picture at Dudmaston. Note the winged flaming hearts embroidered on his collar and cuffs. These suggest he was a Catholic – a dangerous thing to be in Elizabethan England.

There are two pairs of portraits of 17th-century husbands and wives. That over the door to the left of the fireplace may represent Sir Francis Wolryche, 2nd Bt. He inherited the family title in 1668 as the eldest son of Sir Thomas Wolryche and married Elizabeth Wrottesley (the companion portrait on the right), but he never took on the estate, as he lapsed into insanity and was declared a lunatic. Facing one another over the open doors are said to be Sir George Whitmore (Sheriff of London in 1631) and his wife, who were ancestors of the family that inherited Dudmaston from the Wolryches in 1774.

Over the fireplace is a portrait of Anne Miller Christy, painted by Jerry Barrett in 1869, two years before she died. The Christys, like their Darby relations, were Quakers and she is shown wearing the Quaker muslin

The Oak Room

***Skating scene*, by Adriaen van der Venne**

In Holland you are never very far away from water, which turns to expanses of ice in winter. As a result, the Dutch have always been keen skaters. They even invented an icy version of golf, which you can see being practised on the left.

bonnet of the time. She has just put down her crochet.

Furniture

The *chandelier* was bought in 1950 in the Pietersplatz, Vienna, where Sir George was serving in the British Embassy. The Chinese Xianlong period (1736–95) lacquer coffer, decorated with flowers and exotic birds, was brought from the Far East by Captain Henry Bazely, RN, the father-in-law of the Rev. Francis Henry Wolryche-Whitmore.

Sir Francis Wolryche, who inherited Dudmaston in 1668, but was mentally incapable of managing the estate and was declared a lunatic

The Modern Art Gallery, which began life as the family dining room

The Modern Art Gallery

This room is startlingly different from those you have seen so far – indeed from the interiors of most traditional country houses. William Wolryche-Whitmore added it to the house in 1833 to provide a large new dining room, but the Laboucheres decided to transform the space into a gallery for part of their collection of modern British and French art.

Although Sir George was conservative in most of his views, he developed a passion for collecting contemporary art in the 1950s, while serving in the British Embassy in Brussels. He once remarked, 'After going to an exhibition of abstract art I feel as if I have had a number of very good cocktails'.

The artists represented include Ben Nicholson, Barbara Hepworth, Henry Moore, Sonia Delaunay and Jean Dubuffet.

Detailed lists of the works on show are available in the room.

Ceramics

The Chinese porcelain in the two cabinets (AIL) includes outstanding pieces of the Sung (960–1279) and Ming (1368–1644) periods.

> 'I hope the visitors to this display of modern art will not be shocked by an art which may seem unusual to them and that by endeavouring to appreciate a new way of perceiving beauty they will experience the degree of joy and excitement which I myself have undergone.'
>
> Sir George Labouchere

Some of it was inherited and some bought by the Laboucheres after they returned from China in 1948.

The Spanish Gallery

In 1960 Sir George was posted to Madrid as British ambassador. Although the fascist Franco regime was still in power there, young and progressive artists like the members of the *El Paso* group (founded in 1957) were trying 'to create a new spiritual state of mind within the Spanish artistic world'. Sir George bought their work, hung it on the walls of his official residence, and exhibited his collection at the National Museum of Modern Art in Madrid in 1965. Dudmaston remains one of the few places in Britain that you can see examples of mid-20th-century Spanish art.

(Left) Flamenco Dancers; pastel by Sonia Delaunay, 1916 (Modern Art Gallery)

El Cine; collage and watercolour by Antonio Saura, 1963 (Spanish Gallery) (© ADAGP, Paris and DACS, London 2002)

The Botanical Art Gallery Landing

The set of sixteen prints of auriculas comes from C. Oscar Morton's book on this species, which was particularly popular in the 19th century. They were given to Lady Labouchere by the artist Rory McEwen. The print of *Cistus ladanifer* by Mary Grierson shows a sketch of Dudmaston in the background.

On the landing is a portrait of Col. Thomas Weld, who inherited Dudmaston in 1771, having lived here for many years with his sister. On the other wall is a portrait of Isabella Wolryche-Whitmore's mother, Mrs Henry Bazely.

The copper urn came from a Norwegian farmhouse, where it was used to store fresh spring water.

The Topographical Watercolours Gallery

These pictures were collected by Lady Labouchere and bear witness to the many places she visited and lived in with her husband. They range from picturesque views of Dudmaston and other historic buildings in Shropshire, to images of Spain and China.

The Botanical Art Gallery

In her reminiscences of childhood at Dudmaston in the early 19th century, Frances Whitmore recalled that 'my mother and Aunt Dora were good Botanists – I believe Botany became at that period a favourite pursuit of the ladies owing to Dr Darwin's then famed poem of the Loves of the plants'. Lady Lucy Wolryche-Whitmore pressed flowers from the garden and hot-houses, and later generations added new plants and trees enthusiastically. This tradition was continued by Lady Labouchere, who collected examples of work by many of the greatest botanical artists, including G.D. Ehret and P.J. Redouté.

In the 20th century, botanical art was revived by John Nash, whose many pupils at the Field Studies Centre at Flatford Mill included Lady Labouchere, and whose courses were continued by Mary Grierson. Both are represented here.

The Costume Gallery

The displays vary from year to year, because textiles are very vulnerable to light damage. They usually include historic costumes from the 18th century, and cocktail dresses worn by Lady Labouchere in her role as a diplomatic hostess.

Autumn Leaves; by Pandora Sellars, 1975 (Botanical Art Gallery)

(Right)
'The Incomparable Daffodil';
by G. D. Ehret
(Botanical Art Gallery)

NARCISSUS.

The Incomparable
Daffodil.

Charles Babbage (1792–1871) and the Computer

Before Babbage, a 'computer' was a person, not a machine. All mathematical calculations had to be done by hand, aided only by sets of printed tables. The task was tedious and time-consuming, and the results were often wrong. Babbage devoted his life to building a machine that would take the drudgery and the error out of such calculations.

In 1824 Babbage began work on 'Difference Engine No.1', an immensely complex assembly of cogs and axles that would have stood over eight feet high, weighed several tons and comprised around 25,000 separate parts. After nine years' work and little official encouragement, he finally abandoned the machine, having completed only a seventh of it. However, this fragment can still claim to be the first automatic calculator. Despite this disappointment, he embarked on an even more ambitious machine, christened the Analytical Engine, which was designed to be programmed by punched cards. He continued to refine his design, but managed to construct only a simplified version of the machine during his lifetime. Babbage felt that his career had been a failure, but he is recognised today as one of the key figures in the prehistory of the computer.

Like many geniuses, Babbage could be difficult. He was openly contemptuous of the scientific establishment, and was so irritated by the street musicians who disturbed his concentration that he launched a campaign against them. He became a target of ridicule as a result. But he was also a sociable animal. His house in Gower Street, in London, was a meeting place for leading liberal European intellectuals. He numbered among his friends and acquaintances the Duke of Wellington, who arranged an official grant for him, Lord Shaftesbury, Charles Darwin, Michael Faraday and the Brunels.

Babbage is remembered at Dudmaston because of his marriage in 1814 to William Wolryche-Whitmore's sister, Georgiana. He spent a great deal of time at Dudmaston and in Shropshire, often working tirelessly on behalf of his brother-in-law in his Parliamentary election campaigns. The central heating system at Dudmaston was based on that he designed for his own house in London, and he encouraged the 'burning gas' producing plant for lighting, which was in operation here until 1936.

Charles Babbage, computer pioneer
This portrait was painted about 1833, a year of crushing disappointment for Babbage, when he was forced to abandon work on 'Difference Engine, No. 1', which has been called the first automatic calculator.

The Darby Gallery

This gallery shows the connection between Lady Labouchere and the Darbys of Coalbrookdale, as well as the relationship between the Darbys and the Fells and Christys, all Quaker families linked by marriage. On display are exhibits relating to these families as well as to Lady Labouchere's mother and her Wolryche-Whitmore uncles and aunt. At either end, there are showcases of Coalport and Worcester china.

The Old Kitchen

This room is a surviving fragment of the early Tudor house, which was largely demolished in the late 17th century to make way for the present building. It has been much altered since, losing its cooking ranges and sinks in the 1950s. However, the bread oven and the charcoal ovens remain, and also the very large pestle and mortar. The pestle is cut from rock, showing fossil remains.

Implements

The items shown give a glimpse of the domestic life of the past and the staff at Dudmaston. All the copper kitchen utensils, originally placed on shelves around the walls, were sacrificed as scrap for the war effort in 1940.

The wooden fish were carved in Norway and commemorate very large salmon caught there. The fishing rods are of the type used for these catches.

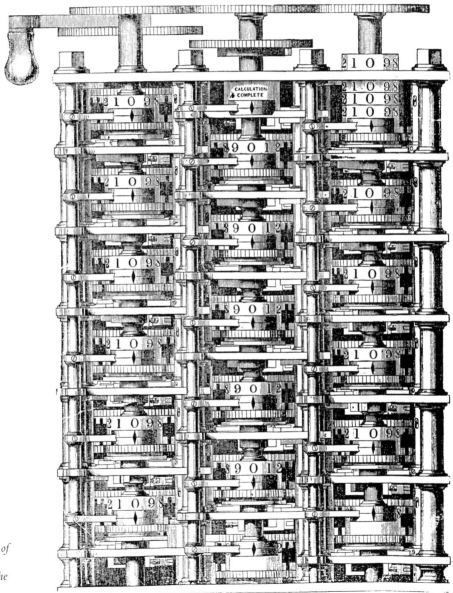

The completed section of Babbage's Difference Engine No. 1, which he abandoned in 1833

The Garden and Park

You approach the house from the Kidderminster–Bridgnorth road through flat parkland grazed by sheep and dotted with specimen trees. This is unremarkable enough. But on the west side the terrain and the mood change abruptly, as the terrace falls away steeply to a string of lakes, with the River Severn and Clee Hill in the distance beyond.

Early history

We do not know what kind of garden surrounded the house when it was first built. The story really begins in 1777, when William Whitmore commissioned a design for the park from William Emes, who had already worked as a landscape gardener at several houses in the West Midlands and North Wales. His plan for 'the intended sheep pasture' was in the open style of 'Capability' Brown. It shows the house surrounded on the south side by a formal orchard or plantation, and with trees dotted about the parkland, which was cut by serpentine drives. Unfortunately, little, if anything, of this scheme seems to have been implemented.

The Dingle

Whitmore turned instead to his wife Frances and to his head gardener Walter Wood, who together created Dudmaston's most famous feature, the Dingle, in a wooded valley to the south-west of the house. The Whitmores' daughter Frances recalled their work:

The Dingle was a pet of our dear mother's. She laid out the walks therein, placed seats and formed cascades in conjunction with Walter Wood, whom she called Planter, and who was many years gardener at Dudmaston and died there. This man had imbibed his taste at Shenstone's Leasowes and the Badger and Dudmaston Dingle were long picturesque rivals. My mother and Aunt Dora were good botanists ...

Wood had worked until 1763 at The Leasowes, William Shenstone's small, but influential garden in the Picturesque style near Halesowen in Worcestershire. The Dudmaston Dingle preserves many similar features: an artfully meandering route past waterfalls, rustic bridges, urns and a hermitage. The flow of water through the Dingle was carefully controlled by dams and sluices.

The garden front of the house looks down over the Big Pool

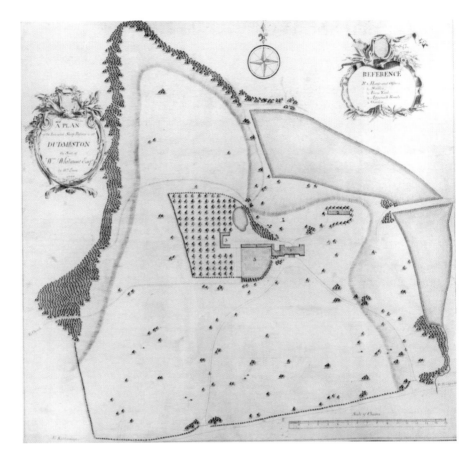

*William Emes's
1777 design for the
park (confusingly,
the north point at
the top actually
points south-west)*

*The garden and park
from across the Big
Pool in May 1793;
watercolour by Moses
Griffiths*

This garden door was decorated in the early 19th century by William Wolryche Whitmore's sister, Mary Dorothea

19th-century formality

Between 1818 and 1850 William Wolryche-Whitmore created the Big Pool below the house by merging three smaller lakes. He introduced more formality by constructing a series of terraces between the garden front of the house and the lake, and by introducing more urns, steps and gravel paths. He also built walls and steps against the red sandstone outcrop, which is now planted with rock roses, heaths, thymes, lavenders and escallonias. This area was restored in 1998 with the support of the National Gardens Scheme. On the south side of the house he dug a ha-ha to separate the garden from the pasture. Here he laid out an area which he called the American Border, as it contained mainly hybrid rhododendrons introduced from the Americas. This part of the garden now contains magnolias, azaleas, Japanese cherries, and a halesia or snowdrop tree. Severe frosts during the winter of 1981–2 killed many of

William Wolryche-Whitmore's original rhododendrons, which entailed rethinking the planting in the American Border. William's sister Mary Dorothea also seems to have been keen on gardening. For she is said to have painted the delightful arrangement of ivy and garden tools on the door now displayed in the garden exhibition.

The 20th century

The water garden in the south-west corner of the Big Pool was constructed by Alice Wolryche-Whitmore and her daughter-in-law Muriel, who planted it with gunneras and bamboo. The small terrace in front of the house was built in the 1920s and the borders below filled with madonna lilies, now interspersed with old varieties of roses.

Planting continued throughout the rest of the 20th century, with Geoffrey Wolryche-Whitmore contributing the *Metasequoia glyptostroboïdes*, one of the first in this country to be grown from seed. Rachel Labouchere made the bed in front of the Brew-house and planted the *Magnolia grandiflora, Wisteria sinensis* and the Spanish rose 'Gava', which she brought back from Madrid.

Like the house, the garden is full of modern sculpture acquired by the Laboucheres, including *Watcher* and *Space Frame*, both by Anthony Twentyman.

The garden today

New planting for the new century includes the climbing rose 'Penny Lane', which covers the wall by the ticket office. The geranium 'Ann Folkard' in the bed below provides an attractive contrast. The nearby honeysuckle 'Graham Thomas' releases a fragrant perfume. The magnolia 'Butterflies', which produces creamy yellow flowers in May and June, has been planted in the American garden. Also worth looking out for here are a small bed of the dwarf *Hydrangea macrophylla* 'Pia' and a lovely deciduous *Ceanothus oliganthus* 'Perle Rose'. A late flowering *Ceanothus* 'Autumnal Blue' climbs over the terrace wall.

The garden in spring

Anthony Robinson's iron gates were commissioned to celebrate the Laboucheres' Golden Wedding in 1993. The Laboucheres filled the garden with similarly adventurous modern sculpture

The Estate

Dudmaston Hall is a solid, sensible house with a Picturesque garden. But what makes the place special is the survival of the historic estate, which comprises 1,195 hectares on the east bank of the River Severn, straddling the road from Bridgnorth to Kidderminster.

Dudmaston takes in part of the ancient Forest of Morfe, which supplied building materials for some of the earliest houses on the estate, such as the timber-framed Little Mose Cottage. Timber was becoming too valuable to use on such humble buildings by the 18th century, when locally quarried sandstone and brick (made in kilns at Lodge Farm) were more popular. Thatch remained the preferred roofing material well into the 19th century, until replaced by Welsh slate brought down the Severn in barges.

The pace of change in this part of Shropshire has generally been slow, but just as the estate was subject to the cycle of the seasons, so it was also transformed by the longer cycles of economic decline and renewal. After a period of stagnation, in 1774 a new young owner, William Whitmore, brought a new, more scientific approach to running the agricultural estate. In the 1780s he enclosed Morfe Heath (the remains of the forest) and improved the fertility of the land by better drainage, manuring and preparation of the soil. He rebuilt Lodge Farm in the fashionable Picturesque style and added new kinds of agricultural building to house cattle and pigs and to store and process fodder more efficiently. New threshing machines brought the benefits of mechanisation to the estate.

Shropshire endured a period of agricultural depression from the end of the Napoleonic Wars in 1815 until the 1840s, when William Wolryche-Whitmore revived his father's investment programme. An ardent campaigner for agricultural free trade, he founded the Bridgnorth Agricultural Society and rebuilt the village of Quatt in red brick. He also set up an Industrial School to train the sons of his estate workers for a life on the land, and the daughters for dairy and domestic work. William Wolryche-Whitmore's free trade policies meant growing competition from American wheat in the 1870s. The result was an even more profound agricultural slump, which the over-mortgaged Dudmaston estate was in a weak position to overcome in the late 19th century. Despite this, Francis Wolryche-Whitmore still managed to find money to build new estate cottages that bear his initials.

Real revival came only in 1908, when Geoffrey Wolryche-Whitmore took on the running of the estate. Having studied the latest methods of forestry management in Germany, in 1910 he planted 200 acres of new woodland and built a new sawmill to exploit it. Astonishingly, until then, all the timber on the estate was still being sawn by hand, by the Earp brothers, itinerant foresters who worked at Dudmaston for three weeks each year. He introduced new species to the woodland and invented new tools such as the Whitmore pruning chisel and the ladder saddle. His work gained Dudmaston a national reputation for forestry management and earned him the Gold Medal of the Royal Forestry Society, and Dudmaston was chosen as an exemplar of the integrated rural estate for the Festival of Britain in 1951.

There are numerous walks across the estate.

A Dudmaston servant with a glass of beer; painted by George Alsop in the mid-18th century (Entrance Hall)

The Dudmaston estate

The owners of Dudmaston

Hanging in the Oak Room is a portrait of a bearded young man, Francis Wolryche (1563–1614). Although this portrait was painted in 1591, when Elizabeth I was on the throne, Wolryches had already been living at Dudmaston for seven generations, having inherited the estate in 1403 on the marriage of Margaret de Dudmaston to William Wolryche of Much Wenlock. The family had been in Shropshire since at least the 13th century.

We have no record of what Francis Wolryche's house looked like, but it was marked on an old map as a fortified manor house, and was substantial, containing 24 hearths in 1673 (only seven houses in the county had more). It seems to have been built in the 16th century on the site of the present house, which may preserve fragments of it in the old kitchens in the south wing. The family seem to have already been prosperous. Certainly, they could afford to commemorate Francis and his wife, Margaret Bromley, with elaborate effigies on their tomb in Quatt church. Their numerous children appear kneeling along the side of the tomb chest – sons on one side, daughters on the other.

Sir Thomas Wolryche, 1st Bt (1598–1668)

The eldest son, Thomas, inherited in 1614 at the age of only sixteen. He was educated at Cambridge University, where according to the inscription on his tomb, he was 'a student of geometry, a seeker-out of Historical Truth, … the kindness he did he ever forgot and but rarely remembered the wrongs that the ungrateful did to him'. In the turmoil of the Civil War, which he lived through, there were many wrongs to overlook.

Wolryche consolidated the estate by marrying a Shropshire heiress, Ursula Ottley of Pitchford, and managed to increase its value tenfold over 30 years. He served as MP for the neighbouring town of Bridgnorth from 1620 to 1625, and like the Ottleys and other leading Shropshire families, was a loyal supporter of the King, who knighted him in July 1641 and created him a baronet less than a month later. When the Civil War broke out in 1642, he agreed to raise a force to fight for the King and the following year was appointed governor of Bridgnorth Castle. In 1644 a Parliamentary army laid siege to Bridgnorth, which the defenders set fire to before retreating into the castle. They surrendered when the besiegers threatened to undermine the castle hill with explosives. The castle was flattened apart from the Keep, which survives, despite leaning at an angle of 15 degrees (far further than the Leaning Tower of Pisa). Sir Thomas himself was fined £730 14s by Parliament – money he failed to get back when the monarchy was restored in 1660. He had

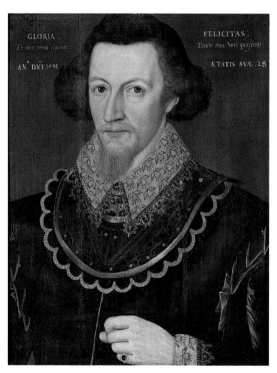

Francis Wolryche, painted in 1591 at the age of 28 (Oak Room)

himself painted in armour with the besieged castle in the background in the portrait in the Entrance Hall.

Sir Thomas's eldest son Francis succeeded to the baronetcy in 1668 and lived to the age of 61, but he proved mentally incapable of managing the estate and was declared a lunatic. The portrait in the Oak Room seems to reveal something of his mental state. Sir Thomas's fifth son John therefore took over responsibility for Dudmaston in 1668. About two years later he married Mary Griffith, the daughter of the chaplain to Charles I and II. In 1678 at the age of 41 she died in childbirth. Her musical gifts are commemorated in the massive monument in Quatt church, which shows her holding a lute. According to the Latin inscription, 'possessing a divine musical talent, she was outstanding as a singer and a player of the lute. On Earth the rival of the heavenly choir of angels, she has now joined them in heaven, their friend and partner'.

In the 1680s John Wolryche began building what was called the 'New House' (now the dower-house) near Quatt church, but work came to a halt with his death from smallpox in 1685 aged 48.

(Right, top) Sir Thomas Wolryche, 1st Bt, who was governor of Bridgnorth Castle (shown in the background) during the Civil War (Entrance Hall)

(Right) John Wolryche, who ran Dudmaston from 1668 until his death in 1685 aged 48. He is shown dressed in Roman armour like his father, Sir Thomas

(Below) Mary Wolryche's monument

Sir Thomas Wolryche, 3rd Bt (1672–1701), the builder of Dudmaston

John's son Thomas had much more ambitious plans. Having inherited the title from his mad uncle in 1689, he married Elizabeth Weld of Willey, from another prosperous local family. He then set about building himself a completely new house. His architect was probably Francis Smith, who came from an industrious family of artisan builders active in the Midlands from the 1690s. Smith had been brought up at nearby Tettenhall, and his brother William was building a very similar house at Stanford in Leicestershire around the time that Dudmaston was constructed. The family of Sir Thomas's aunt Elizabeth Wrottesley also employed Francis Smith to build Wrottesley Hall in Staffordshire in the 1690s. The best evidence for

Sir Thomas Wolryche, 3rd Bt, the builder of Dudmaston Hall; by Richard Gibson

the attribution is a letter of 10 April 1695 from Sir Thomas's father-in-law, George Weld, to Andrew Archer of Umberslade Hall, another early Francis Smith house very similar to Dudmaston:

Having had ye hon[ou]r to sit with you in the House of Commons makes me soe bold to beg of you that if you have a moddell of your House you will lend it to Sir Tho: Wolryche my Son in Lawe for some time, and I will carefully Returne it to you againe, if you have not such a moddell, that then you will lett this bearer take a platt [plan] of ye same.

Smith offered reliability and convenience rather than stylish sophistication. The model for his country houses was Belton in Lincolnshire: a simple H plan with a central entrance hall and saloon, flanked by identical three-room cross-wings. The red-brick exterior and the plain sandstone window surrounds accented by miniature keystones are typical. Inside, the spacious, panelled Entrance Hall has changed little since Smith's craftsmen completed it.

The 18th century

However, Sir Thomas probably never saw his new house finished, as he died suddenly in 1701 aged only 29 from a combination of jaundice and TB. He left a ten-year-old son John in the care of his widow Elizabeth, who managed the estate in partnership with her brother, Col. Thomas Weld. The house may not been completed for some years, because Elizabeth was living in London in 1705. It may have been here that John picked up the bad habits that were to destroy him and almost wipe out the estate. While he was still a minor, he could be held in check, but in 1712 he came of age and for the next eleven years he led a life of extravagance. His account books record the large sums he spent on horse-racing, hunting and cock-fighting. He was more anxious about losing his dogs than his money. A collar tag from one of his hounds is displayed in the Staircase Hall. It is inscribed: 'Pray Return me to Sir Jn. Wolrych Bart. At Dudmaston'. The end came on 25 June 1723. After celebrating too well a winning day at the Chelmarsh races, he was drowned while trying to ford the River Severn on his way home in the early hours of the following morning.

Dudmaston was left with crippling debts and no male heir. Eventually, a complex legal settlement was reached whereby the estate passed to John's sister Mary for a payment of £14,000. This was a period of retrenchment for the estate, but there was enough money left to restore the family church at Quatt, which was given a new tower, nave and north aisle in 1763. Their mother Elizabeth remained in residence in the house, eventually outliving her husband by 64 years. With her brother, Col. Weld, she continued to offer traditional, if slightly frugal, hospitality to their guests through the 1750s:

Dinner was ready every day at one o'clock for twenty persons, and when the Bell rang any neighbouring Farmers out working in their fields were welcome to come and any friends of the family who chose to partake of the plain hospitable dinner provided. Those who came in time sat down with Colonel Weld and his sister Lady Woolridge [sic], those who were late partook with the servants and after all had dined the remains were given to the poor …

When prayers were over, they went to dinner. The Colonel brought always a bottle of wine from which you were expected to drink one glass, if you took more, it was more than was expected, or desired, but there was plenty of Ale. When Lady Woolridge was able to come into Company, she went after dinner to a closet in the room and brought a bottle of port with her from which you were likewise asked to have one glass.

Life was rather quieter in the 1760s, as Lady Wolryche was blind and bedridden for her last seven or eight years. She eventually died at the age of 92 in 1765. Her daughter Mary never married and when she died in 1771 left Dudmaston to her closest living relative, Col. Weld. The inventory of the contents of the house taken on the Colonel's death in 1774 records huge quantities of linen, and a well-stocked kitchen and wine cellar, but the main rooms seem to have had little in the way of grand furniture or pictures. The Entrance Hall, for instance, was furnished with only 'A Small nest of drawers, a table, a screen, a Clothes Chest with drawers'.

The Colonel, who had no legitimate children, left the estate to a distant cousin, George Whitmore, who came from another ancient Shropshire family, with estates outside the county at Lower Slaughter and Appley. George outlived the Colonel by only a year, but his son William brought a new family and fresh energy to Dudmaston, which had been in quiet decline for more than half a century.

The Wolryche Hunt, on which the wayward Sir John Wolryche, 4th Bt, spent large sums in the early 18th century (Entrance Hall)

A new start

William Whitmore (1745–1815)

The new owner of Dudmaston was a young sailor from Southampton with an eye for the ladies. His daughter described how he met his first wife, Frances Lister:

[He] was not a man long to remain a bachelor having a true blue nautical love for petticoats. He butterflied among the Lady Greys at Enville and I know not when but was attracted at Shrewsbury Races by a Brunette and a Blonde. The Blonde however carried the day.

The young couple had to start by refurnishing Dudmaston, as it had lost most of its Wolryche contents:

My father found Dudmaston a large and in some parts unfinished house quite empty. I have heard him say he could find nothing when he took possession – but an old pair of yellow breeches in a large antique oaken chest – which I remember. He said to his Housekeeper Mrs Harling – I suppose I shall want a few things in your line look about and get them – Want a few things in my line Sir, why you want but everything in every line.

Fortunately, he had also inherited estates at Leebotwood and Woolstaston which gave him the resources to put things right. In 1776 he spent £466 on new furniture and £432 on repairing the house, which may have included adding the hipped roof shown in Moses Griffiths's watercolour of 1793 (illustrated on p. 19). He also reinvigorated the long-neglected estate (see p. 22).

The nursery gradually filled with children, as, with increasing desperation, William and Frances tried to produce a son (only a male heir could inherit the estate). At the seventh attempt, in 1787, a son, William, was born to much ringing of church bells; but Frances died five years later, after having given birth to another three daughters. The elder William remarried Marie Louisa Thomas, and their son John went on in 1828 to inherit the beautiful Jacobean house at Chastleton in Oxfordshire (now also the property of the National Trust).

William Wolryche-Whitmore (1787–1858)

A contemporary described him as 'a fine, tall, formidable man', and he left his mark both on Dudmaston and the political landscape of the times. In 1810 he married Lady Lucy Bridgeman, a daughter of the Earl of Bradford. Four years later they set off on a continental tour, which included visiting Napoleon in exile on Elba, who assured him that the French 'despised almost all other nations except the English'. They returned to take up their inheritance in 1815 on the death of William's father, when he added the old Wolryche surname to their own. William also inherited the family's traditional parliamentary seat at Bridgnorth, but expounded views that were far from traditional, arguing for Catholic Emancipation and the repeal of the Corn Laws in a stream of pamphlets. His radical opinions did not go down well in Shropshire, and so in 1832 he stood for the newly enfranchised urban seat of Wolverhampton. He was elected, but only after a bitterly fought campaign. The eulogy

William Wolryche-Whitmore, who revived the Dudmaston estate in the early 19th century

inscribed on his monument in Quatt church acknowledges the personal cost of these political beliefs:

He saw the evil of restrictions on the free importation of food and year after year in his place in the House of Commons he laboured to effect their repeal. Repeated defeats by large majorities, the faint support of friends, the reproaches of his own class failed to daunt him in the faithful discharge of this public duty.

In the 1820s he commissioned a local builder, John Smalman, to remodel the attic storey with pediments at the corners and dormer windows to light new bedrooms for his numerous visiting relations. On the ground floor, he created a large new library and dining room, and installed central heating designed by his brother in-law, Charles Babbage (see p. 16) in an effort to make the house more comfortable for his wife, who was in delicate health. Large sums were also spent on modernising the estate, but the result was to saddle his successors with outstanding mortgages of £60,000.

The Wolryche-Whitmores had no children, and so left Dudmaston to their nephew, Francis Laing, in 1858.

Rev. Francis Henry Wolryche-Whitmore (1820–1908)

Before inheriting Dudmaston, the Rev. Francis Laing had been rector of Quatt church, where his loud preacher's voice was put to good use, and he seems to have had mixed feelings about taking on the heavily mortgaged estate. One of his first economies, in December 1858, was to sell the contents of the cellar – '300 dozens of first class wines'. For the next seven years Dudmaston was let out to an Australian sheep farmer, and only in 1864 did Francis decide to change his surname from Laing to Wolryche-Whitmore and move into the house. According to his grandson, keeping the place going through the agricultural depression of the 1870s

A bust of the musical Lady Lucy Wolryche-Whitmore stands by her harp in the Staircase Hall

brought him 'a life of worry', but by 1900 he had managed to pay off the mortgages.

His grandson described him as 'a dear old man, absolutely unselfish, fond of a joke, and his great joy was to have some fresh person for dinner with news or information of some kind.' The food provided by Mrs Shepherd the cook was plain, but plentiful. After dinner he would snooze with the newspaper in the Library. An impressive beard almost hid the fact that he liked to pull off his uncomfortably stiff collar and tie in the evenings. His grandchildren were put up in the attics, where they would make soap slides along the oak passage. His own chief recreations were game and rabbit shooting, and fishing for pike in the lakes. The woodlands were managed for sport rather than timber, and the gardens kept in good order.

After his wife Isabella died in 1902, he retired to live with a sister in Tewkesbury, and passed Dudmaston on to his son, who was also called Francis.

The early 20th century

Francis Wolryche-Whitmore II had started out as a lawyer, but his wife disliked living in London, and so they decided to return to Shropshire. When he inherited Dudmaston, he was already in his late 50s and happy with the life they had made at Larden Hall. So, once again, Dudmaston was let to a tenant, for whom acetylene gas was installed in 1908. Francis himself lived here only from 1912 until 1921, when he returned to Larden and handed over to his son. But although his time at Dudmaston was brief, he established connections, through his marriage to Alice Darby, that were to bring many beautiful and fascinating things into the house. Alice's father was Alfred Darby, whose family had pioneered the smelting of iron with coke at nearby Coalbrookdale, making it the crucible of the Industrial Revolution. Her mother was Rebecca Christy, who commis-

sioned the leading Arts and Crafts architect Norman Shaw to build a country house at Adcote in 1879 and filled it with French furniture and Chinese porcelain, some of which is now at Dudmaston. Her Christy uncles were all distinguished in different ways. William Christy founded the hatmakers of that name. Henry Christy invented the modern bath towel. In the late 1840s he visited the sultan's palace in Constantinople, where he discovered loop-pile 'Turkish towelling' in use. With his brother Richard, he developed a method of producing it by machine, and displayed the results at the 1851 Great Exhibition with immediate success. Henry was also a pioneer anthropologist, and left his important collections to the British Museum in 1865.

Francis Wolryche-Whitmore's son Geoffrey trained as a land agent on the progressive estates at Apethorpe and Buscot, and in 1908 at the age of 27 he took over responsibility for running the Dudmaston estate. Over the next half-century, he made Dudmaston a model of modern estate practice, especially in forestry management.

Geoffrey's first wife Susan died in 1907 after less than three months of marriage, and his second marriage, to Muriel Murray, was childless. So in 1952 he passed Dudmaston to his niece Rachel.

Dudmaston transformed

Rachel, Lady Labouchere had two lives – firstly, as a diplomat's wife; secondly, as the last chatelaine and creator of modern Dudmaston. She met her husband, the diplomat Sir George Labouchere, while she was working at the Admiralty in 1942, and they were married the following year. They made a pact: she would follow him round the world on his diplomatic career, and on his retirement they would make a home at Dudmaston. So for the next 24 years they travelled to postings in Sweden, Nanking, Buenos Aires, Vienna, Budapest, Brussels and finally Madrid, where Sir George served as British ambassador from 1960 to 1966. Some of the outfits worn at the numerous diplomatic

Rachel, Lady Labouchere, who devoted her retirement to transforming Dudmaston; painted in a Hartnell gown in 1962 by Ricardo Macarron (Staircase Hall)

receptions she hosted are shown in the Costumes Gallery.

In 1966 Geoffrey Wolryche-Whitmore moved out of Dudmaston, and the Laboucheres settled in, having commissioned the interior designer Nina Campbell to redecorate the interior. Lady Labouchere had inherited Dudmaston on the understanding that it would eventually be given to the National Trust (a process completed in 1978), but she and her husband transformed this gift in many ways. They ensured not only that one of Shropshire's oldest traditional estates was preserved as an entity, but also that the house and garden were filled with things old and new that would surprise and delight visitors. So Old Master flower paintings, furniture and porcelain that had belonged to her Darby and Christy ancestors are displayed with 20th-century works of art collected by Sir George (see p. 12).

With unstoppable determination and charm, Lady Labouchere campaigned for the creation of the Ironbridge Gorge Museum Trust, one of the first and most imaginative industrial archaeology projects, and she served as its president for fourteen years. She also wrote books on Abiah and Deborah Darby, and masterminded the exhibition about the Darbys of Coalbrookdale at Dudmaston. Lady Labouchere became a keen gardener and botanical artist, having trained at Flatford Field Studies Centre with John Nash and Mary Grierson, whose work is represented among the botanical displays in Gallery Four. The Laboucheres marked their Golden Wedding in 1993 in a typically adventurous fashion, by commissioning a set of new gates from Anthony Robinson.

Lady Labouchere died in 1996, and Sir George in 1999. They had no children, but their memory lives on in all the many things that they did for Dudmaston.

Lady Labouchere's cousin, Col. James Hamilton-Russell, and his wife, Alison, continue to live in the house.

THE FAMILIES OF DUDMASTON

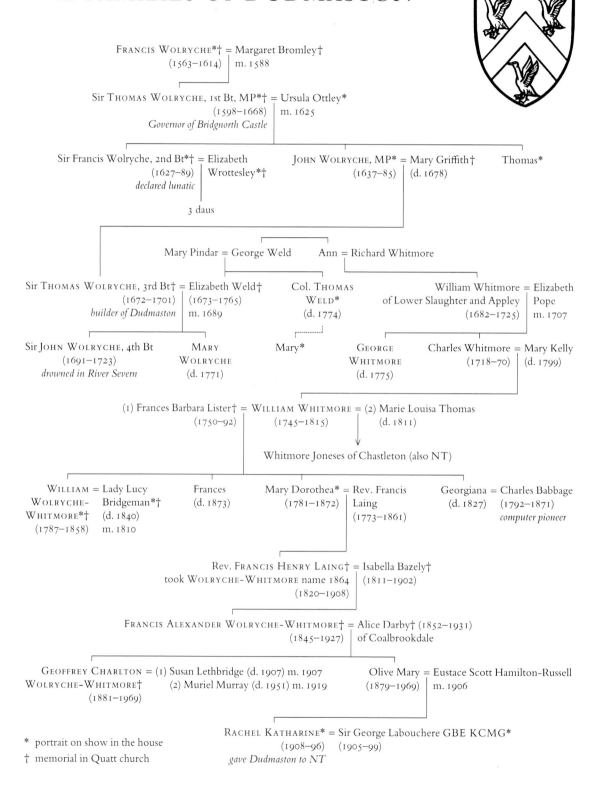

FRANCIS WOLRYCHE*† = Margaret Bromley†
(1563–1614)   m. 1588

Sir THOMAS WOLRYCHE, 1st Bt, MP*† = Ursula Ottley*
(1598–1668)   m. 1625
Governor of Bridgnorth Castle

Sir Francis Wolryche, 2nd Bt*† = Elizabeth   JOHN WOLRYCHE, MP* = Mary Griffith†   Thomas*
(1627–89)   Wrottesley*†   (1637–85)   (d. 1678)
declared lunatic

3 daus

Mary Pindar = George Weld   Ann = Richard Whitmore

Sir THOMAS WOLRYCHE, 3rd Bt† = Elizabeth Weld†   Col. THOMAS   William Whitmore = Elizabeth
(1672–1701)   (1673–1765)   WELD*   of Lower Slaughter and Appley   Pope
builder of Dudmaston   m. 1689   (d. 1774)   (1682–1725)   m. 1707

Sir JOHN WOLRYCHE, 4th Bt   MARY   Mary*   GEORGE   Charles Whitmore = Mary Kelly
(1691–1723)   WOLRYCHE   WHITMORE   (1718–70)   (d. 1799)
drowned in River Severn   (d. 1771)   (d. 1775)

(1) Frances Barbara Lister† = WILLIAM WHITMORE = (2) Marie Louisa Thomas
(1750–92)   (1745–1815)   (d. 1811)

Whitmore Joneses of Chastleton (also NT)

WILLIAM = Lady Lucy   Frances   Mary Dorothea* = Rev. Francis   Georgiana = Charles Babbage
WOLRYCHE-   Bridgeman*†   (d. 1873)   (1781–1872)   Laing   (d. 1827)   (1792–1871)
WHITMORE*†   (d. 1840)   (1773–1861)   *computer pioneer*
(1787–1858)   m. 1810

Rev. FRANCIS HENRY LAING† = Isabella Bazely†
took WOLRYCHE-WHITMORE name 1864   (1811–1902)
(1820–1908)

FRANCIS ALEXANDER WOLRYCHE-WHITMORE† = Alice Darby† (1852–1931)
(1845–1927)   of Coalbrookdale

GEOFFREY CHARLTON = (1) Susan Lethbridge (d. 1907) m. 1907   Olive Mary = Eustace Scott Hamilton-Russell
WOLRYCHE-WHITMORE†   (2) Muriel Murray (d. 1951) m. 1919   (1879–1969)   m. 1906
(1881–1969)

RACHEL KATHARINE* = Sir George Labouchere GBE KCMG*
(1908–96)   (1905–99)
gave Dudmaston to NT

*   portrait on show in the house
†   memorial in Quatt church

32